Death Tractates

Death Tractates

Brenda Hillman

Wesleyan University Press
Middletown, Connecticut

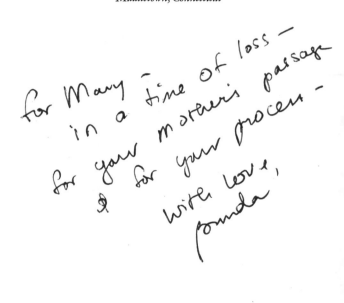

for Mary — time of loss —
in a time of loss —
for your mother's passage
& for your process —
with love,
Brenda

Published by Wesleyan University Press, Middletown, CT 06459
www.wesleyan.edu/wespress
© 1992 by Brenda Hillman
All rights reserved

Printed in the United States of America 10 9 8 7 6 5
CIP data appear at the end of the book

Originally produced in 1992 by Wesleyan/University
Press of New England, Hanover, NH 03755

ISBNs for the paperback edition:
ISBN–13: 978–0–8195–1202–4
ISBN–10: 0–8195–1202–8

Grateful acknowledgment is made to the following magazines for printing some of these poems: American Poetry Review *("Much Hurrying," "Near Jenner," "Reverse Seeing," "A Dwelling," and "An Entity");* Berkeley Poetry Review *("First Tractate");* Pequod *("Possible Companion," "Split Tractate," and "Black Rose");* Ploughshares *("Sideways Tractate," "Keeping Watch," "Divine Laughter," "Subtle Body," and "Finding Her");* Zyzzyva *("Yellow Tractate"). Many thanks to Joe Ahearn, Fran Lerner, and Carol Snow for their advice, to John Prendergast for his guidance, and to Bob Hass and Louisa Michaels for being close by.*

Contents

A Note about the Book

At the beginning of 1989, my closest female mentor died suddenly at a young age. I had been working on a manuscript to be called *Bright Existence*.

The poems in this little book presented themselves as "an interruption" to the other work (though the themes and sources—many of them gnostic—are similar); I tried to will them to be a part of *Bright Existence*, at first allowing them only a certain number of lines, twisting them to fit assignments. But they would be written only when/as the present form showed itself to me (like a butterfly opening out on a leaf).

In this process, the relationship between the two books changed as well. Though this book was a sister to the other, it still needed to break away, to stand by itself.

February 1989–January 1990   *B.H.*

FOR LMP

1947–1989

On the day that I am nigh unto you, you are far away from me.
On the day that I am far away from you, I am nigh unto you.

—from a gnostic identity riddle

Calling Her

First Tractate

That the soul got to choose. Nothing else
got to but the soul
got to choose.
That it was very clever, stepping
from Lightworld to lightworld
as an egret fishes through its smeared reflections—

through its deaths—
for it believed in the one life,
that it would last forever.

When she had just started being dead I called to her.
Plum trees were waiting to be entered,
the swirling way they have,
each a shower of
What.
Each one full of hope,
and of the repetitions—

When she had been dead a while
I called again. I thought she was superior somehow
because she had become invisible,
because she had become subtle
among the shapes—

and at first she didn't answer; everything answered.

Tell now red-tailed hawk
(for we have heard the smallest thing cry out beneath you):
have you seen her?
(Red hawk) Thrush walking up
the ragged middle:

have you seen her? Mockingbird with your trills
and scallops, with your second mouth
in your throat of all things
tell us:
where is she whom we love?

I closed my eyes and saw the early spring,
pretty spring, kind of a reward;
I opened them and saw the swirling world,
thousands of qualified
pinks, deer feeding
on the torn changes

and I wanted to go back 'from whence' I came.

Up the coast,
along sandbanks and spillways,
the argued-about bays, spring came forth
with its this 'n' that, its I can't
decide, as my life had
before she died: preblossoming:
cranesbill, poppy—

and I wanted to go back "from whence" I came.

Heart that can still see our heart
Heart that will not let us rest

February evening—
young mothers in the drugstore with valentines
all of which needed to be used.
Packages of plain or lace ones

stuck together. And the mothers
proud of themselves for remembering,
the valentines slumped down so the red
merely looked promising
but pressing up bravely anyhow—

the awkwardness of what's here,
ceaselessly trying to arrange itself;

I went out in the night, I called out,
I felt along the edges of the panel:
without her,
everything seemed strange to me in this world;
just the taste of oranges: imagine!

And all of this compared to her seemed bulky.
For weeks this was true.
As if only being dead were the right amount.
Only being dead were fragile enough
for what the earth had to say.
Clumsy. For a while. Clumsy. For a while
it was too much to go on living.
Roadside acacias—
I could not bear them. All unzipped,
like meaning.
The ostinatos of the birds.
Magnolias—dogs'-tongues—curved
to spoon up rain. Too much shape.
Even that which was only suspected
of having it: the iris
that lay in the ground with their eyes of fate.

And then the other voice said

You who long for things
who can't understand borders
who like to spread your magic and your blame
forgive yourself.

She'd given you an impossible task:

she said to follow and you intended to.
But you'd come to a place in the forest
where there weren't any tracks—

Much Hurrying

—So much hurrying right after a death:
as if a bride were waiting!

Crocuses sliced themselves out
with their penknives. Everything well made
seemed dead to them: Camelias. Their butcher-
paper pink. The well-made poems
seemed dead to you,

only what was vastly overheard would do,

you had to say something so general
over the edge
that everyone could hear—the guests,
the bride—though the edge
was specific to you, the edge was inside—

Secret Knowledge

At first I was able to speak to her quickly
just by closing my eyes.

She had died in the first week of quinces,
when things put forth their secret knowledge:
fiery, random blossoms are allowed to live,

and robins don't seem all that common
as they swing at the tops of cypresses
through new song;

and I wanted to hear just one voice
but I heard two,
wanted to be just one thing, but I was several;

I called her more quickly,
told her how much I missed her,
pausing at the edge of the screen

that kept me from her
in all the awkwardness of living,

and she said it was not up to me
to live without her
or make the voice be single,

she said every voice is needed.
Every voice cries out in its own way—

Holding Her

—Then the owl came back the druid the helper
and you asked,
Where is she whom we love. Who-who,
it said, who-who, matching sets
for you and her—

you who had sought distinction
in the pronouns
found they were all the same—

but wasn't that death a gift to you as well,
just as the life had been?
Now you got to hold her
by yourself, for the first time—

Near Jenner

I asked the mind for a shape and shape meant nothing;
I asked the soul for help, and some help came:

some wedding-band gold
came around the edges of a sunset,
and I knew that my bride could see forward, behind it;

and all the women I had known
came back from their positions
where they had been hanging the silk
laundry of heaven
upside down by the elastic;

they'd help me find her

though they looked slightly faded from being dead,
as the first wildflowers here—
radish, and the ones they call 'milkmaids'—
look faded when they appear
on the shoulders of the Pacific—

Visiting Creature

—You think about a poem too much.
Like Spanish moss,
it starts killing the tree!

Look: Berkeley spring. A mockingbird
has chosen you. Try to follow his new
short songs: buree, buree, cheat-sheet, and the one
that sounds like maybe I
will and maybe I won't do any such thing.

Each time the gray feathers on the throat part
it looks like another mouth
as though the song came from that.

But you? Your friend has been gone
such a short time
you can't keep her voice in you yet.
Who is noticing her now? What is this to her?

So many shifts in that bird's style—
yet what a pleasure to watch him
getting drunk on juniper berries,
resting lightly on his wing bars.

Pretty soon the borders won't bother you either.
Pretty soon your loved one
will speak forward: into this world—

Seated Bride

She had died without warning in early spring.
Which seemed right.
Now that which was far off could become intimate.

I said to the guides, let's stand
very close to the mystery
and see how far she's gone
and whether she is still our bride

(imagining no one fails in this)

because of the sense I had
that she sat parallel to us.
Not above, or below: beside—

The Panel

—No, the upper heavens wouldn't do;
she couldn't manage stairs. Why not
keep her here,

just separated off a little bit?

So you thought of the moment of death
as a kind of panel or screen
behind which she might
join the watcher

and the watcher
did not change. Phenomena
streamed by in circles,
and the watcher did not change—

but no. That heaven was boring
and besides. What lived
lived on both sides. What lived

went back and forth: across the panel—

Writing Her

Yellow Tractate

Smart daffodils! They waited
till the cold snap was over, then brought themselves
into the corridor, like lamps of pity—

they'd help me find her.
Well, actually . . . I didn't want to.
I wanted to be
What.   Lost in her.   Infinitely
lost in her dead life so my life no longer showed;

but I feared I couldn't draw the line around her, then!

Spring swelled sideways, its yellow crescendo,
tall mustard flowers, warblers
the same color;
spring opened like autobiography
and everything shimmered from the inside
out till there were three
types of endlessness: life
death or both which was what she was:

endless. That frightened me.

So I studied the lines around the daffodils,
wanting to see how they could be
and not be at the same time,

die at the right moment as she had
then go on living with force, exactly as she had said.

But anything that had a shape
was cheating her.

A minuet. The dresser
for example. An afternoon

at the DMV—such shape! The living
have such shape in them!
The official taking the multifoliate forms
and pressing down with his ballpoint
hard, harder, and the pen
maintaining smooth shapes for him.
Patient people in line with their hats and scabs and skin
holding them in as they watch
each letter being made—
no wonder conquerers come forth!—and outside
in the parking lot
where the cars are being tested by young drivers
spring draws its yellow crayon around everything.

What shall be safe from the anguish of borders.
Can Monday? No. Sunday
smears forward into it.
Can March? No. February pushes
because its yellow has already started.

And the poems:
things kept getting into them.
Sometimes the poems were active and dead,
sometimes alive and not active, like my friend—

One day I watched a Japanese lady
working the gift-wrap counter. The regular
was sick. The sample gift wraps
all lined up above her

and I noticed that, in its separateness,
each sample seemed to hold its own surprise,
like minutes,
though the boxes of course were empty:
"Wedding," "Birthday," the masculine
sportsman's type of gift wrap
with crossed rifles and golf clubs
and the paisley princeton type—I thought,
these boxes do their jobs
because they have borders;
I need some too.

The lady took such central care to curl the ribbons—
took her about twenty minutes really—
I loved her hands as she debated
how to put the foolish little windmill on
(that broke my heart.
The insistent shining of it
whirling around on the red stem)
and all I could think of as I watched this whirling was
Where is my dead one?
Shape makes life too small.

But I needed borders to do the remembering,

needed them to get the package out of there.
Who would get the package out
if I had no borders. I needed them
in order to be anything at all—

Reverse Seeing

—A fox ran across your path—pure totem!
You would never see it again;
likewise the loved one:

you stared hard into the rusty aftermath.

But things kept coming through the panel of death:
doves took off
outside the window: click click click,
(click)—gosh, their wings needed oiling—then

no more them!

You want to be like your dead friend?
You are like her. Writing
is dying. But the war
was not about borders it was about surrender—

Possible Companion

The mockingbird stayed for months in the legustrum—
blips and screams,
I couldn't get a thing done;

and though I know control is an illusion
I'd go outside and talk to it
in the sort of shallow sun.
Week after week of helping it along
in the powdery white tree
like helping the new kid in seventh grade—
that awkward mix of sympathy and greed
that always rises from the deepest place—

and I thought I could help my dead friend too
though her new dead voice was terribly full

but I feared I was controlling her even in heaven;
that her voice had had to be stopped
for me to speak at all;
that death did not subtract, it added something,
her death made me whole—

A Dwelling

—And in the central valley,
people were dreaming of peaches.
Starlings ate the scalloped edges off new blossoms.
In the night orchards,
the dreamer walked over hot coals with the poems
and made creation seem effortless—there!

What do you fear in a poem?

(I fear the moment of excess, as in March,
when oxalis comes out all in one day.)

What do you fear in the poem?

(I fear that moment of withholding—
especially inside what I thought was free;
and I feared the poem was just like her,
that it would abandon me—)

—So the poem is the story of the writing of itself.
In the white tent of the psyche
or out there in the normal fog:

the mockingbird all spring:
she looked just like a note herself,
each bit of music slipping past her
till it stopped—
each time one note missing;
it wasn't exactly failure on her part,
she just needed something to do tomorrow.

Same thing with the poem. Perhaps
an idea came with it, an idea of fourness, the yellowness
of spring, a certain belief in the completion
of a plan. Not so now. In your dream
of wholeness, death began.

So, put yourself in the way
of the poem. It needed your willing
impediment to be written. Remember the lily,
growing through the heart of the corpse?
You had to be willing to let it through the sunshine
error of your life,
be willing not to finish it—

Losing Her

Split Tractate

But I feared that her soul didn't
miss me. Didn't miss spring. That she was pre-
occupied, like a tourist, maybe not
moving around in the mind
of god but in the onyx
market, which was the exact same thing—

Help, mockingbird! don't say no!
Maybe she has forgotten us,
she has given us this priceless gift,
she has let us go.

I looked for her in anger,
behind sunsets,
along the iron tracks of the personal;
I looked for her in planes of agony
and she was quite close by.

They said I had to let go of her.
She said so too. Let go she said from the
What.
The screen between me and her.

But still I held on; holding on
is my specialty. I held on to her image,
to the moment of death, to the problem
with pronouns; maybe I'd learn.

Spring could let go couldn't it.
Vireos hung upside down from the cottonwood.
The old calm towhee at the feeder—it did not tarry.

Beautiful, average mornings: the scattered actual: grief
changed them only slightly.
Mornings waiting for the triple A,
of neighbors standing by their cars and chatting,

one pink kleenex
in the street—or is it a camelia—

then a man climbs up the shining ladder to a phone pole,
takes the spool of insulated wire and threads it—
Where?
To the heaven of messy souls
behind the bright new consciousness
or to the old Baptist heaven with its silverware—
so many heavens! Which was she in.
I wished she'd speak more clearly when I asked her
who was noticing her now.
What was "this" to her.

And the mockingbird stayed all morning with its row
of checkmarks and the verse that sounded like
teacher-teacher-teacher
police! police!
Maybe that bird was her—
so versatile; it did not cling—

let go said the
What.
Let go said everything

Sweet afternoons of exhaustion. Trips to the library
with the other moms. Taking the books

to the chrome mouth of the book deposit
and hesitating
before letting the slender paperback slide down
on its very own bardo journey;
Maybe I should have warned it
not to attach itself to its travels,

not to identify with the suffering,
that is the main thing.

What is this so-called
death anyway. Fat chickadees hop up
the "dead" fennel. A little
cowlick sprouts from the 'dead' place
in the pine. Petals die
and in a day, what looks like mascara brushes
fall from the birthday tulips.

Is the falling or are the tulips *it*.
What is this so-called
death what is it.

Let go said the so-called
What.
Let go said everything.

Even the poem said it.
Said it would come in its own good time
as I leaned forward to see death's face
though there was always this gap
between my hand and the page,

I had only to trace the pen
over the words;
the poem was already written—

Random Order

—Don't you see?
It doesn't matter what order you put them in.
It only matters that you started them,
got yourself to love this new non-
being as it were.

This fear of being away from her,
of being away from her body
even for an hour—

did the starlings forsake the orchards
though they dwelt elsewhere?
Each time they brought their need it was so different—
such randomness! They flew in
with their delighted throats
then, they gave themselves over to it—

An Entity

When she was about to die he said she had been visited
by *an entity*. Had been urged,
he said, to cross over to the other side of the—
O.K. Whatever.
This dark helper, like my Magdalene,
smart, gypsyish, was not dismayed
when my friend hesitated.

I think of this quite often now.
This striving for perfection
in the art, against my will,
this being caught up in the lateral sense
of the divine and heaven
(compared to the up-there kind)
is probably due to the fact that the entity won.

I know my understanding is being completed day by day.
But in my grief, I made it a contest;
the entity and I pulled at her
from our separate sides,
like the women in Solomon with the baby;
I knew I should let go to prove I loved her more
but I wanted her all to myself. And maybe,
I thought this pleased her—

Winged One

—Not unwillingly, but not with lightness either,
not sure of itself
but with great hope in its energy,
the mockingbird still sat there at the end of spring,
speckle-sided, flapping its wings up high,
stealing whole passages, like a young poet—

and what it could not discover
it was taught: break the rules
with your singing, don't be normal, shatter the plot.

You think her voice collided with yours?
All right. The voice collided.

But, what if the outside voice wasn't true?
What if, despite your false calm,
your brokenness, your self-deception—
in fact, when you were most broken,
her heaven was you?—

Finding Her

Sideways Tractate

, , , all morning. I looked
for that bird all morning and never found it,
just heard , , , all morning
from the dripping cedar,

death as comma,
as interruption,
the warning that the rest of the sentence would follow,

then in the house next door
someone dusted the piano: tuh-dee, tuh-dee,
tuh-dee, tuh-dee, then stopped
and played "Here comes the bride"—

Spring kept coming forth. I love that word.
So much comes forth instead of up:
the cardinal crests of the rose thorns, the floppy
ears of the sorrel,
things I'd been able to tend on this earth;

I thought if I could get to her
I'd tend her also. My black rose.

Baffled. For a while. Baffled. In the end
I couldn't get to her.
I looked between the rows of books, between
grief's "stages"—
they lied, of course; grief has no stages—

her face came from the general background
not being looked for
but being found.

For several months I spoke to her.
She even moved her mouth and all.
Some will say this is memory but it is not memory.
I simply looked across the row of days
to what she had become—

a little wild around the edges,
shining, unavailable,
across the serious spaces.
Across! Such an odd direction. Not like the men,
who travel "up" or "down"—
across.
So instead of the descent into hell
it seemed I had learned death
by looking sideways.

I didn't fear the center of her death,
I feared its edges,
the part that did not need me any more,
that pushed out, like some stubborn little galaxy
as if the shape she had made
for a lifetime didn't count , , , that "life" for her—
padding about in her slippers
outside the bedroom door, where I last heard her,—
that the life I remembered was simply
an interruption,

the moment when the principal shine in matter
can, for a brief time,
be made fitting,

and what was I now in relation to her.

But I remembered how things advance in other worlds
if they are sufficiently loved
and I sought to 'advance' her, even in heaven—

My my my my. A few months
then the face faded. First the edges
then the center.
I longed for her because she had turned away
toward what did not include me.
I longed for her
though I understood what important work she had,
though I knew she was "very busy"—

Keeping Watch

—So the soul had known it all along,
the soul knew when it was taken:
first it filled with light
and then it went
sideways, through boxes of radiance;

you wanted her to look your way
but she couldn't;

for the bride can't just stop
being the bride
once the forward exit has begun,
going backward would have hurt too much.

So you had to
What. Choose
whether to call out as she passed by.

The choice was simply
whether to live in 'memory' and time
or outside—

Divine Laughter

She used to talk about divine laughter.
I took this one of two ways.
That the soul would be laughed at
even in heaven,
not kept out of the silver net exactly
but as when the women at a school meeting laugh—
at, not with,—when they don't know
how to enter your condition.

But the other kind I heard was (this):)
in the ripples of fat in the clouds over Bolinas:

neither silence nor the little hissing click
some shorebirds make when they land
but that combination—

the egret so like a bride, the bride so like an egret
who comes in, who lets the great shimmering
take over! And I began
to know what she meant by the magic, spreading—

The Guides

—You asked the day once more but it had not seen her;
you asked the night for help, and some help came:

Christ came, and Mary, his little dark pet,
and John with his cup of staggering—
they'd help you find her
among what had not been transformed;

you who have no borders,
who can't understand echoes,
hadn't you noticed all along?
Where there was nothing, now there was everything.

That they came to you again and again
bearing your grief as a huge white flower
full of sweets and gold
as if it were no work for them at all!
they carried it lightly between them
and their arms stayed straight—

Subtle Body

When she had been dead all spring I called again,
remembering the beings in the texts
who get to spin around in both worlds;
I wanted to see if what had been hers
was still hers,
if what was mine, was mine;

she appeared in one of the gold rings
they use to keep the faces certain
on the other side.

I read that when the body
begins to disperse going back
it gives off something that looks like gallery dust—
I noticed a little of that
over to the right;

and I reached through it
because of the love I had for her;
I thought she would try to reach back
but she had already

What.
She had stepped out of the way
of deciding to decide—

Finding Her

—The mind asks the question;
the heart is hurt by the unknown;

you didn't have to take care of the dead one
for she could still love
what came forth
though it seemed to you like suffering—

too hard for you?
Listen. You don't have to do anything.
The raccoon is in the garbage can, selecting an eggshell;
there's a patch of moonlight
on the rug. Get up, stand in it, be seen through—

And out in the night
where the ragged patches converge:

everything that lets go
still has its memory of attachment
and that which refused to let go
still has its uses—

Black Rose

—You asked for the difference between life and death.
Safe in your non-death,
you exposed yourself to an answer.

So you were surprised
that the earth was warmer than you thought,
fueled as it was by the central joy,
and at the moment of your question,

you were handed,
like a black rose, the paradox—

Quartz Tractate

Let's see now. The idea of reverse seeing:
whereby a plant will be seen for instance
by the ground. My friend saw backward into this world.
In the tent, where wisdom is eaten
by the snake, the poem sees into us.
Days and nights of this;
the job of the living is to be seen through.

As a swallow, harrowing the raptor, dives
in and out of the forbidden ovals,
seeming to derange them,
only to realize the raptor doesn't care,
goes on with its crenellated flight,
so I entered the mystery
and the mystery ignored me—

Baffled by death, I sought her in myself,
sometimes—often—speaking to her.
Now that has faded a little—

But still.
Why doubt that she goes on helping?
We were both everything in this. It wasn't
that she was the crystal and I was the ashes.

I go to the hill where "she" lies and see
it's true. Things borrow splendor.

In the shine off the back of a very large beetle
on the driest hill where so much is in bloom.
Even the serpentine pebbles in the cracks bloom,
even the cracks bloom.
The beetle crawls across one and goes on
lifting its legs as high as it can—

Library of Congress Cataloging-in-Publication Data
Hillman, Brenda.
    Death tractates / by Brenda Hillman.
    p.   cm. — (Wesleyan poetry)
    ISBN 0–8195–2199–X. — ISBN 0–8195–1202–8 (pbk.)
    I. Title. II. Series.
PS3558.I4526D4   1992
811'.54—dc20   91–22257
∞